she fits inside these words

she fits inside these words

r.h. Sin
Samantha King Holmes
Robert M. Drake

Andrews McMeel
PUBLISHING®

chapter one
by r.h. Sin

It's late where you are, the night sky a grayish concrete blue. You're here every night, aren't you? Alone beneath the stars, the moon, your night-light. There are moments when you almost believe that sleep will come easily, and it should because your heart is weary, but your dreams are further than you'd hope. It's after 10, and you've already begun counting how many hours of sleep you'd get if you fell asleep now, but come on, you're kidding yourself. Midnight happens way too often for the heart that deserves rest. And you bear witness to those lonely hours every fucking time. And maybe it's a pain inside you that has brought you here. I wish I could promise some fashion of salvation; I want nothing more than to be the author of everything that helps you heal, but I am nothing but a stranger to you, and so maybe these words will not reach for you in the way I intended. And still, I yell to you to keep running toward whatever helps you stay alive. May the night sky find the light of the sun so that you might have another chance to spark joy.

———————————

I'd wait up all night just to witness the midnight showing of your heart. And even while you're draped in sadness, you are the most beautiful thing my eyes have seen. So strong and resilient. So courageous and capable. Everything you need to be to survive the darkness that arrives when the sun is no longer visible. And when it's all said and done, you'll stand beneath a full moon, patient for the setting sun.

You are a manifestation of the truth being told in a room of liars. You outshine the sun, and you captivate the soul of whoever dares to stare within your eyes. You tell stories with every move you make; you are a walking representation of survival in motion. You fit best in the night sky, a child of the moon. A myth until they meet you and witness, for the first time, a flower with the strength to bloom in the dead of winter.

Your eyes are always so sad in every photo you post, even as you smile. There's a picture-perfect sorrow whispering from your face. Sometimes I wish I were sitting in front of you, as if to say you're not alone. Of course, you have someone, or maybe they just have you, and you're still trying to prove yourself worthy of their attention, but they continue to neglect you. Is that him in the photos? Is that the person you pretend to be happy with? You're reading this right now because you're unhappy with him, right? I'm sorry, I don't want to come off as rude; I guess I care way too much about something that has nothing to do with me, but that won't stop me from saying all of this to you. Isn't that why your eyes are fixated here? You're searching for a sign or a reminder or some courage to do what should be done.

Surrender to yourself. Surrender to the woman in the mirror looking back at you with sad eyes and a broken heart. Do what she needs you to do to save her. Let go, move on, and save yourself.

I have been searching for you while being distracted, seeing someone who was never the one I should have been chasing, and you were doing the same. The saddest days of my life committed to a relationship filled with lies. I was starving for the truth that only you could feed my fractured heart—struggling to stay afloat, reaching for the hand that didn't deserve mine. How often did we miss one another while claiming to love someone else? How badly could I have wanted to be loved while staying stuck in a relationship that resembled the prisons of hell? We lose so much time holding on to lovers who hate us. Living day by day but going nowhere. Both of us in spaces where we don't belong. Why do we make each other wait for love?

Hell was the relationship that kept you broken, and I know you feel the urge to text him back, but when the devil calls your name, you need not answer.

He's gone, but you still have yourself. He hurt you, but the heartache made you stronger.

I'm not telling you to stop singing; I'm just trying to let you know that not everyone deserves your song. And you don't need to turn the volume down; instead, play those melodies loudly for yourself.

I hate the way I fumbled my heart into your hands. Losing sleep over you while you spend the night with someone else. I've lost track of all the hours I wasted minimizing my own emotions to be considerate of how you feel, and that was foolish because you've proved time and time again that you've never given a fuck about me. And I hate the way I could muster up the courage to care for someone who was never brave enough to fall for me.

It's like you're waiting to be loved, but you're not even single. You're taken, but you're alone. Smiling while your eyes scream out in sadness, and there's an emptiness in your laughter that only I can identify. Or maybe you know this as well, but you've chosen to play pretend, ignoring your reality. Fighting back the tears just to appear happy. It's like you're waiting to be loved while pretending to be in love with the one person who will never be the one you've been waiting for.

Samantha, a summer rose, a chill of air in the winter. My springtime; I'm sprung. I knew I'd fall, and beside you, I fell. And when they ask me what I loved most about being here, you are the story I'll tell.

I'm confident that there is beauty behind that mask that hides your scars.

———————————————

Your heart is a sanctuary, the way you have me on my knees. I'm thankful for whatever led me to you and the salvation in your love.

_____

Look at yourself with loving eyes. Everything you've longed for has lived within you the whole time.

Your heart was never meant to carry this sadness, even though it can, and your shoulders weren't made to carry the weight of the world, but you can, and you have. And maybe that's why I care so much about your happiness and peace. I think I'm just tired of good women getting hurt by people who were never worthy of their time, energy, and love.

––––––––––––––––––

You are a never-ending ocean with no shores, and so you've learned to find a home within yourself.

———————————

Don't tell me ghosts aren't real when I can see you but you're obviously no longer here.

—————————————

When your heart is feeling something that your mind is tired of, that's painful.

Staying makes no sense, but you hold on because you can. You tolerate the suffering because you're used to mistreatment. And maybe you're ready for something different, and you're just stuck between the floorboards of a home that no longer feels safe and a front door that is actually the exit. Daring yourself to leave, eager to break free.

This fire didn't·hurt her; it forged her power.

There will be days dark as night and summers when you feel cold. There will come a time when being strong means admitting that you're hurting. And your lips will no longer pretend as they give way to the tears in your eyes. Feel what needs to be felt, and learn from all the things that break your heart.

Some relationships never even begin; those are the hardest to end.

If your heart is leading you to someone who doesn't care, reroute and search for directions to yourself.

It rained, and she wasn't looking for an umbrella. She was searching for inspiration.

I didn't want advice; I didn't want a solution. I just wanted you to hug me. That was it, and one day you'll read these words, and you will have realized that you were too late.

Being with the wrong person will have you doubting your potential.
Being with the wrong person will have you questioning the effort
and devotion you deserve in a relationship.

_____

I felt it, the moment we began to lose one another. And every day after felt like the earth being pulled apart slowly from the center.

It's not that your love isn't good enough. I think, early on, we are taught to give love to those who appear to be without it. What they don't tell you is that loving those types of people can leave you damned and doomed for heartbreak with the realization that they are incapable of appreciating it and they don't intend to give it back.

———————————————

Be gentle with your hands as they search for one to hold. Be kinder to your heart as it looks for someone to love.

You deserve someone who tries every day to be deserving of you.

You left, and I grew stronger without you. Thank you.

There's a universe of inspiration living inside her bones, and it's a shame that you never made time to explore beyond her surface.

––––––––––––––––––––––––

Her eyes melt the stress in my heart. Her touch quiets the static in my head.

Just wait. There is someone in this world who is ready to love as much and as real as you do.

I hope you find the one person who will name a star in their heart's constellation after you.

You will learn to live without him when you learn to love yourself.

_____

It's like you're trying to forgive yourself for all the shit that he did to you. That's not right.

The silence was always the loudest coming from you. And even though there were no words, I understood everything you wouldn't say.

―――――――――――――

It's strange; my heart is heavy and empty all at once.

Crazy to think that I was hoping you'd silence my demons, but they were you all along.

A part of me hates the idea of finding true love later in life. There's this fear that what we have for one another will somehow not be enough after the world has had its way with our hearts.

———————————

You've been wasting those restless 3am's on the wrong person.

_____

We were silent, so pain spoke in the absence of our words.

No judgment here, but how can someone have so many lovers and still feel so unloved. A phone full of numbers and still feel so alone. Social media full of likes and still feel like shit.

———————————

There's a brokenness in your smile; there's a sadness in how you manipulate your expression to make others feel like you're okay even when you want nothing more than to feel like your pain is acknowledged. You sit there, hidden away with your secrets. Yelling in silence, crying behind a smile, but I hope you know that you're not alone.

I know they describe love as a spark or fireworks, but to be honest, I felt a bomb of emotion going off in my heart and throughout my bones when you touched me.

Fully dressed, I made her feel things. We made love before we could even touch.

———————————

You're the flavor of the future I wish to taste.

_____

I think I fell in love with her soul first and the well-being of her heart. With her body still a mystery to me, I wanted to spend whatever time she'd give me proving that I was deserving of her presence.

Women need to know that being cheated on is no fault of their own. You can't blame yourself for someone's inability to comprehend the value of the love you've shown and the devotion you've given.

————————————

You can't find love in a man who is comfortable with being heartless.

_____

Too often, you've felt yourself losing people who were never even yours to begin with. How painful is that?

———————————————

The trouble with love is that sometimes you find yourself falling
for people who will eventually leave with every empty promise they
made with your heart.

Most men use the word "beautiful" as a key to unlock everything they don't deserve to access. And I think that word would lose its meaning and power over you if you truly knew just how often he's thrown around that word with others.

———————————————

I don't think the pain leaves entirely. You just learn to fade fragments of heartache by drowning the sorrows with what little joy you can create.

Why was I so willing to believe in you when you did nothing to earn that belief? I gave you the best parts of me, even when I felt wronged. I wrote you into chapters of my life, even when you did nothing worthy of being drafted into my story. Why did I continue to make time for someone who continued to waste mine? I opened up doors for you to places you could never enter on your own, but all you wanted to do was piss me off and waste time on your phone. I risked everything to see us through, but you were never present enough to notice. Taken for granted, neglected, and made to feel as if nothing I did was enough. My shortcomings were the only thing you could acknowledge, as if you were blind to all the times I tried my best and did what was right. And here I am, using up letters to create words to describe why I'm wasting the alphabet on you. I hate the idea of love destroying our mind's eye ability to see the truth. I can't stand the way I was whenever I was next to you. My dreams transformed into nightmares, and so I dared not sleep. Thinking I'd lost my heart to you, but it was never yours to keep. What happens to love when it fades behind what could have been? And is there even an opportunity to heal when the scars are this deep? I guess I'll never know until I go and go on some more. I think the answers have always been hiding in your absence, and in the ending of what I thought would last, there will be clarity and closure waiting for me on the other side of us.

And so sometimes the end doesn't have to be bitter. A relationship ending is a painfully sweet reminder that the best is yet to come. On your way to this realization, there will be bumps in the road, and it won't be easy, but I can tell you from experience after experience that either you will find the right one or the right one will find you. It takes courage to leave behind people who fail to love you, it takes courage to detach from relationships that feel more like dead ends, and you will be brave enough whenever that time comes. The end will show you that you can begin again and with someone better, someone who will genuinely appreciate the love in your heart and soul.

I keep thinking about how people hold on to their phones as if they are genuinely a part of their being; in fact, I believe that this device has become more important than the people it promised to help us all stay in contact with. The problem is that we use this device as a way to stay connected. It's actually destroying our connection with others. What if instead of reaching for the phone, you reached for yourself and or the person you claim to love so much. Is it too much to ask for, the request for relationships, friendships, and family time that isn't disrupted by this urge to check for notifications that ultimately mean nothing in the real world? There are times when I miss the moments that weren't interrupted by the call to fill those moments with whatever you could find on your cell phone.

———————————

Roses die quickly without being nurtured, and so did we.

You should always forgive the cheater for their choice to betray you. A decision they've made that is rarely a mistake, if ever. You should forgive the cheater while refusing to allow them back into your life. The forgiveness is not for them; it's for you. Forgiveness is one act of kindness for yourself as you move on without them.

Forgiveness is not to be used as an excuse to take them back, nor does the phrase "I forgive you" mean that what they did was somehow acceptable. I can't remember how often I wasted second chances on people who didn't deserve an opportunity to even hurt me to begin with. Or how often my forgiveness was taken for granted and used against me. You can forgive a person and not allow them the chance to hurt you again. You can forgive a person, not because they're sorry but because you need to tie up any loose ends before you walk away. Forgiveness is most often closure.

———————————————

Most breakups are opportunities to discover new beginnings. They may hurt for a moment, but you will find the courage to begin again.

Too often, you've found yourself struggling to walk away from people who have already left, and I hope that it is this realization as you read these words that you somehow figure out that what is already gone was never worth being kept by you in the first place.

You had to get hurt to become a stronger version of the warrior you've always been.

———————————

Be a mess when it's over, if that's how you really feel. Fall apart, if that's what is in your heart, but no matter what you do, never run from the truth of what your heart wants to express.

The other day, I walked by a restaurant window, and in a brief moment in passing, I witnessed two people at a table and one holding their phone while the other watched with sorrow with a look that screamed, "I wish you smiled at me that way."

Some words live deep within you long after being screamed toward your heart by the people you thought would stick around forever. And though they're gone, you can still hear their voice breaking you down whenever sadness finds you.

I like to think of you when my skies are gray; there's just something about envisioning your face that makes this shit feel okay. Your eyes are like portals to what joy I need. Once locked away by sadness, but with you, I'm free.

For days now, my mind has cultivated reasons to think of you. Wanting only to be alone with you, as if to say with my silence that I am here whenever you're ready to speak. I am always prepared to listen. Your every breath the inspiration I've searched for in people who weren't you. I'll be honest, I've lied to myself. I whispered I love yous without truly knowing what they actually meant. And sadly, I've played my part in wasting the attention of lovers I couldn't love for the simple fact that I have always been at odds with loving myself. But there is something about the way you smile that makes me curious about what happiness can be found in spending time with someone with the grace and strength that you embody. For days now, my mind has made new excuses as to why I wonder about you as you wander through my thoughts carelessly with the fresh eyes and opinions of someone who could be considered radical in this day and age. There's courage in your tone, a stride in your walk that resembles someone who has gone out in blizzards and made it to the other side of the storm. You have scars, but nothing you're ashamed of, as you wear those markings as proof of your survival, and I admire that about you. The way you've bundled your issues and obstacles together and set them ablaze just to keep yourself warm. For days now, I have found myself being in awe of you.

I don't think building a wall is a sign of weakness. I think it's best to protect yourself from the things that don't deserve to get close to you, and sometimes being hurt helps you see the red flags clearly so that you can begin the process of removing an entry point to your heart.

Listen, I know you hate being alone, but that is never a good excuse to waste your presence on people who don't deserve to be in your company. And maybe it's none of my business. Perhaps I've ventured into a territory that I don't even deserve to navigate, but I'll take my chances to reach you with these words. I know you want to be loved, but how can this ever happen if you refuse to choose yourself over those who have decided to disappoint you? These words are written with the intent of reminding you that you have more than enough of what you'll need as you leave behind unhealthy relationships, friendships, and family. Keep moving forward if it's love you're after.

let it die, let it die

let the truth waltz inside

watch it set fire to the lies

witness the pain as it perishes

within a blaze of glory

let it die, let it die

the idea of you and i

———————————

There's an entire library of everything you don't say left collecting dust on your heart shelves.

The men who fail you the most will want you to be perfect.
The friends who lie will always want your truth, and the family
members who want you to be the bigger person will never apologize
or own up to the wrong they do or the pain they've caused in your
heart.

———————————————

You try to leave, and they beg you to stay, but when they're ready, without warning, they'll easily walk away.

It made ruins of my heart, loving you.

Stay and stand barefoot in these fields full of battles you've yet to win. This world would be too quiet without the sounds of your battle cry.

There is a girl who still knows that she is deserving of every ounce of love she's lost in others, and I hope her eyes are moving left to right on this page right now.

She's the girl you write about when you reference heaven. She's the one on your mind when you think of bliss. She's you.

———————————————

She's been running from the chaos of loving the wrong person for a while now, and with each step she gets closer to peace, closer to herself.

————————————————

The old man told me to chase my dreams, and maybe this is why I'm here writing about running after you. I know you've suffered in the past and your heart is not ready to love again, but I'll wait because you're the vision of what I wish my future to be. So when you're ready to choose someone other than yourself, choose me.

I imagine that you spend your nights searching through your memories for something worth remembering. Playing back at all kinds of moments in search of something that'll make you smile, and maybe this page of this book can be added to those endless rolls of pictures you take with your eyes. And when you feel alone, you'll revisit this moment and recall these words written to you. There is a love that lives in the air of the night, and I hope it finds you whenever you need it the most because you are deserving of something that'll make midnight easier.

———————————————

What belongs in your life will never leave you. And anything that drifts away was never worthy of holding on to. Remember this.

Love of my love, you deny me by holding on to him. And you don't recognize my face while distracted by his. We miss each other because you're missing someone who will never love you like I'm willing to. I write your name in the night sky with my fingers, hoping that you'll notice while looking for the moon. Am I a fool for wanting the same love you wasted on him? Am I wrong for believing that I could be right for you while I write to you? Patiently I wait outside a locked door to which only he has the key, but there's some hope that you'll change the locks or, better yet, you'll leave then run toward peace with me.

chapter two
by R.M. Drake

WHEN MY BROTHER LEFT EARTH

I swear,
if I would have known,

I would have slowed time
just to be with you

a little longer.

I would have dropped everything
I was doing,

and I would have been
with you all night.

If I would have known,
I would have prepared

better words.

Better words to comfort you.
To save you.

To help you realize
how important you were.

I swear,
if I would have known,

then perhaps
you'd still be here.
You'd still be alive.

Still be wandering the earth.
Making sense of all those things

we would talk about
when we were young.

I swear,
if only I had known

that week
was going to be your last week.

If only
I had known that day
was going to be your last day.

Your last moment.
Your last cry for help.

If only.

Imagine that, my sweet brother.
Imagine where you'd be.

Maybe you'd still be here with us.
Smiling.

Laughing.
Drinking.

You know, being you.
How sweet would that be?

To heal your mother's heart.
To revert everything

that has changed.
Imagine that, my sweet boy.

Imagine that.
If only I had known,

I know
I would have saved your life.

As if my life depended on it.

WHEN PEOPLE BECOME OBJECTS

I wanted your love,
but all I got was your pain.

I wanted to believe
that we were okay.

That we really had
a chance at love.

A fair shot, you know?

I really thought you were the one.
I really thought

you were it.

That what we had ahead of us
was what we were meant for.

You know they say
that a part of us dies

when you lose someone you love.

That a part of us
gets buried alive.

Gets taken away from us,
and from that moment on
we are never the same.

Never meant to feel
the same things

with other people.

Never meant to forget.
I wanted your love.

I wanted your trust.
I wanted to be a part

of your soul.

But in the end,
all I got was your pain.

And maybe that within itself
was a lie.

Sometimes I feel
like I never really got a chance

to spend time
with the real you.

Like I was in love
with someone
I wasn't meant to meet.

Someone I thought
I knew.

Someone I lost
a few moments

before we even met.

WHEN YEARS PASS US BY

I read a headline
on December 26th of 2019,

and it said,

"The year is almost over.
And all we could think about

is the way we've learned
to survive.

The way we've learned
to let go."

This is true for all of us.
This is religion to our souls.

We learn.
We live.

We laugh and we cry.
Every year, we grow.

Every year, we get closer
and closer to becoming

a better version of ourselves.
Every year, we get wiser.
We get more compassionate.
We get closer.

We find new things
that speak to us.

We discover hidden gems
about ourselves.

Every year, this happens
to all of us,

no matter how hard things get.

We grow.
We learn.
We adapt.
We survive.

And somewhere in between,
we share love.

We share those holy parts
of ourselves

with the people
we care about most.

This is how we survive.
This is how we learn.

This is how we come together.

How we find
what we deserve.

How we let go
of what we don't.

WHEN WE DON'T SAY NO

Happiness is hard
to come by.

People who are real with you
are hard to come by.

Love is hard to come by.
True friendship

is also
hard to come by.

So it makes no sense to me
why good people

get fucked over the hardest.
Why good people

have to go through it
in the worst of ways.

I don't understand
why people hurt them the most.

Why people are so careless
with the ones who show them

soft, gentle love.
Why people are so senseless
to the ones who make them feel alive.

by R.M. Drake   97

To the ones
who genuinely want to help them

find their happiness.

For the life of me,
I don't understand this.

Why people are so cold
to those who care.

Why people act so cruel
to those who reveal themselves.

To those who are too real with them.
To those who show them the way.

I don't understand it,
and I probably never will.

It's just something *that happens*.

Something the ones
with the biggest hearts go through.

It hurts to know this.
It breaks my soul

knowing

that the people who care
the most

end up feeling
what they don't deserve.

End up dying a little slower.
End up always breaking

a little harder.

Than most.

WHEN THE SUN RISES

There are more
than just flowers

in your heart.

More than just stars and galaxies.

Your heart is the beginning of it all.
Where your world begins.

Where it stops.

Pay attention to the way
you bloom.

The way you give birth
to your light.

Your magic.

Pay attention to the way
you love.

To the way it matures and grows.
Pay attention to yourself.

To what you feel.

To what makes you whole.
Pay attention to your heart.

Do not silence it
out of shame.

Out of fear.
Do not cover it up

to fit in.

To be a part of a certain crowd.
Do not mask what hurts.

Do not control what you love.

There are more
than just flowers

growing out of your heart.
More than just stars and galaxies.

More than just life and breath.

Pay attention to your heart.
Do not let it drown.

Do not let it fade in silence.
Give in to it,

but *really* give in to it.

Mean it.

Follow it.

Just don't let it kill you.
Don't let it run you toward the ground.

Don't let it lead you toward
the wrong kind of people.

Toward the wrong kind
to love.

Always pay attention
to your heart.

But always
do not let a minute go
by doing something else.

Believe me,
anything can happen.

Anything.

There are so many ways
to lose yourself,

but don't let your heart
be one of them.
Don't let it be the cause.

Pay attention to the flowers
in your heart.

Water them.
And let them become more.

Let them be
what makes you heal.

WHEN THE FOLLOWING YEAR IS YOUR YEAR

I hope next year
you stop expecting things

from others.

I hope you stop
expecting people to change.

To be something they're not.
I hope next year

you come to terms with this,

that people are·
the way they are.

That no amount of effort
can undo what they've done.

I hope you start doing things
for you, and I hope

you take the steps you need
to move on.

To forgive
the people who've done you wrong
but to never forget
the way they once made you feel.

I hope you take
what you've been through this year

and learn
how to tell the difference

between what you deserve
and what you don't.

I hope next year
you get closer

to everything that moves you.

I HOPE YOU GET
ALL THE THINGS

YOU LOVE.

WHEN TWO PEOPLE ARE ALONE

She asks if things get better.
If things ever clear up.

And if things ever sort
themselves out.

I take my time when I answer her.
You know I don't want to give

her a lazy response.

I take my time with her.
I am patient with her

as I would like her to be
patient with me.

I pause.

Turn the television low and breathe.

"I think things do
eventually get better," I say.

"Or maybe they don't get better,
and it is we

as human beings
who adapt to harsh conditions.

For example,
you know when you are

in love with someone,

almost always
do you overlook the bad.

You condition yourself
to terrible behavior.

Meaning
eventually things do get better,

but it is only because
you think they are getting better.

Because you've thrown in the towel
and you've given up.

You've blocked out
what hurts.

You get used to it."

She laughs
and grabs the remote.

She then turns the television's volume
back to where it was.

"I think you're on to something."

"I never really thought about it like that," she says.

"Well, maybe it's because you've conditioned yourself to think otherwise.

You think things have gotten better.
But, hell,

maybe they have not," I replied.

WHEN THE WORLD TELLS YOU WHO YOU ARE

Just be yourself.

That's all
everyone really wants anyway.

To meet real people.
To meet people who genuinely care.

Who genuinely want
to listen to what you have to say.

That's all we could hope for.
To be real with one another.

To be true
to what we feel.

And hope
someone understands us

for who we are.

And hope
someone accepts us

and shows us
the kind of love we deserve.

So be yourself.

by R.M. Drake   109

Don't try to be anything else
but that.

Wear your heart on your sleeve.
It's okay to do so.

Be real with yourself.
Be real with the people you love.

Be kind.
Be good.

Be open to trying new things.
To learning new things.

Just be yourself.

Don't try to be more.
Don't try to be less.

WHEN YOUR FRIEND IS A SUPERHERO

Sometimes having someone
sit next to you

without having anything to say
is all you need.

Someone who just knows
what you're going through.

Someone who's been there before.

Who knows
what it is like to fall

into their own void.

Sometimes
there is no amount of words
in the world that could ease

your soul.

Sometimes
the only thing that can save you

is the warmth
that comes from another person.

That comes from
someone who stays.

by R.M. Drake   111

That's why best friends
are hard to come by.

They're diamonds in the rough.

They sit with you
when you need them the most.

They say everything you feel
without having a word to say.

WHEN YOU LOSE WHAT YOU LOVE

Sometimes you can't fake it.
You can't ignore it.

When it's real, it's real.

And what hurts is
how you do everything in your power

to move on.

To move forward,
but in the end,

none of it really works.

In the end,
all you really do

is dig your own grave.

You never quite
get over them.

You never quite
get far enough to lose them.

They sort of linger.
They follow you around
everywhere you go.

They become ghosts.
They become scars.

They become that one person
you wish you could go back to.

That one person
you wish you *still had*.

Sometimes it works out,
but sometimes it doesn't.

But none of that matters.

When it's real, it's real.
No matter how much time passes.

They'll always be
the one who got away.

The one you remember
when you come back home.

WHEN YOU SEE IT, YOU WILL KNOW

If you feel it
in your soul,

then let it in.

Let it mend your brokenness.
Let it heal what hurts.

Let it become
a part of your soul.

Amen.

WHEN YOU LOVE WHAT YOU SEE IN THE MIRROR

It is not selfish
of you for wanting to be loved.

For wanting to be cared for—wanted,
 you know?

And it is not arrogant of you
for knowing your self-worth.

For knowing what you deserve.
It just means

you know exactly what you want.
You know exactly

what you need.

Who to let in.
Who to let out.

I cannot emphasize this enough.

Self-love is that one relationship
you have with yourself.

The one that never leaves you.
The one that grows

as time goes on.

And to be honest,
there is nothing more beautiful than that.

Nothing more meaningful.

The fact that you could possibly
fall in love with yourself

year after year
and not have to worry
about what others think.

Not have to impress anyone
or do things you don't want to.

Loving yourself can do that for you.
It can give you the protection

you need
when no one is willing

to step in.

chapter three
by r.h. Sin

In all my years of living, I've reached the understanding that anger moves the body backward; it keeps the heart stuck and makes the soul restless. And I have begun to forgive others; not to say that I have been okay with their mistreatment of my time and energy, and I haven't forgiven them to make space for them to continue to live within my life. I see forgiveness as an opportunity to broaden the horizon of my own life. I view forgiveness as a passageway to put more distance between yourself and those who hurt you. And so, I forgive you.

How beautiful it is to find someone who hears the music in your soul and the value in your presence. Someone who willingly listens to your stories but can also appreciate the moments of shared silence. Someone who wants nothing more than to support your peace of mind.

Her softness came from the same place of her strength. Her beauty defined beneath the surface. The essence of everything she was could not be seen with the naked eye, only felt by those who dared to look deeper. And you missed it because you were never brave enough to know her honestly.

Hell can arrive in the form of people pretending to love you. And this type of hell happens too often to the hearts that need a little bit of heaven on earth.

Crying is the heart's way of taking action to empty itself to make room to feel something other than sorrow.

Do not exchange being alone with the loneliness of being with someone who hurts you.

The betrayal of a friend is like the moon abandoning the night.

———————————————

A friendship that fails was always fraudulent to some extent.

———————————

Some friends only have your back because they intend to stab you there.

Stop going out into blizzards for people who make it snow in your heart.

A true friend will never lead you down a path of roadblocks. A real friend will never keep your mind and soul from evolving.

Sometimes losing friends means making room for the right people.
Sometimes losing a friend gains you the clarity you need to find
your way back to yourself.

You forgive strangers faster than friends who hurt you because you expect nothing from those you don't know and everything from the people closest to your heart.

In a way, you're a flower because of the simple fact that most people will never truly comprehend and or understand the value of your presence until the feelings you felt for them fade.

You can love a person for years, and they'll never show up for you like the person you've known the least amount of time.

It's hard to move on when you're stuck with the idea of what you're leaving behind. But what waits for you will more than likely be better than what will live in your rearview mirror.

A friendship buried beneath a rumor was never meant to survive, and the hardest part is that you only realize this after the person you loved has chosen to allow the lies from others to overshadow your truth about yourself.

Relationships require truth, and there is nothing but lies on his tongue.

The problem has always been weak men making firm promises that appear full but are still empty of what you truly want and deserve.

I was once in a relationship with the wrong person, and this is what I felt, and maybe you've felt the same way about someone you've been with, and perhaps you feel that way right now.

It was hell holding on. It'll be hell letting go.

Some of it was okay, but the rest of it was old gum. It was faded of flavor, dead in its own right. Deserving only of being spat out.

first stranger

then ally, lover then a foe

now enemy and soon

you'll mean nothing to me

―――――――――――――――――

Let go of the hands that do not move to prove that they are deserving of feeling the warmth on your skin.

——————

It never needed to be perfect, and I just wanted to feel like I mattered as much as you did to me.

Nothing will hurt more than the discovery of a friend who was always an enemy in hiding.

The most powerful person in the world right now is reading these words with eyes that have been sad for far too long.

Furnish the spaces of your heart with only the people who have done enough to show you that they belong there.

You've been lost in search of yourself, and you'll realize that you fit among the words on these pages. Your heart draped in darkness lit up by the moon as the clouds move slowly across the sky like a haze of everything you wish you could forget. You don't remember what it felt like to live, as you've never loved the wrong person, and so here you are in search of something that I'm hoping I can help you find. I don't have all the answers, but maybe here I'll be able to provide some clarity.

I do not wait to be loved; I am my lover.

We were together but distant in what we felt for one another.

———————————

Loving someone doesn't justify the torment they cause in your heart.

_____

The broken heart is emptying itself of everything that shouldn't stay.

Poetry in motion is a woman setting fire to everything she no longer wishes to keep.

Summer visited her every year, and the sun stayed around longer, reaching out for her skin.

Wrap your arms around yourself and cover your body with love and strength.

I'm sorry, but I wish to interrupt you from that sadness you've been feeling. Stumbling through the day as your legs grow weaker and your shoulders ache from carrying around the weight of all the painful interactions you've had with people who chose to hurt you.

Your heart begins to break, and the pieces you leave behind will lead the right person to you. Just be patient.

You were always this way, and I just decided to ignore it. I masked your inconsistency with what I hoped you'd become. I made excuses for you, which prompted me to stay longer than I should have. I believed that things could be better, that you could change, and that we could grow, but time would prove you to be untrue, and with time I learned to stand without you.

You've been trying to force truth in a bed filled with lies, which is why you can't sleep, guided by a temporary lust that will never become love.

Maybe it isn't the wrong time. Perhaps you're just with the wrong person. We make any excuse to stay, and we fight against logic and reason. Fooling the heart into believing the lies it's been told. Maybe they're not the one, and perhaps it's time to go.

———————————————

I could have found life with you, but all this time, you were just another deathbed for my tired, aching bones.

This should come as no surprise, but I'm leaving you. I'm walking away so that I can find reasons to feel joy outside of the despair you caused within my heart. You painted me blue with every disappointment, and you buried my smile with every lie you told. I unfolded myself for you, unpacking my heart, and kept it open, hoping it would make a difference, but you refuse to change. And though it should not come as a surprise, you'll be shocked to know that, in your absence, I will be able to discover everything you made seem so complicated. I'll replace you with all that I am, and that alone will be sufficient.

———————————

You're never the same after they've betrayed your trust, and the irony is that they'll want you to remain as you were, even though they didn't appreciate it the first time.

You are a poem expressing itself through heartbreaking truths; in the end, there is peace.

The pain will die, and joy will live within you again.

You settle because you feel like you are not enough. You don't see how you shine during nightfall, and you have no idea that the day only exists because the sun is trying to match the way you illuminate each morning and afternoon.

———————

Try harder for yourself, especially when others refuse to try for you.

———————————

The nights are that much darker after you've had your heart broken.

Our relationship was hell, but you were heaven in my dreams.

The hardest part about leaving is trying to figure out what should be left behind and what is worthy of being kept.

I think nightclubs are just shelters for the lonely.

———————————

If you're not the main character in his story, rip your name from his pages.

You have to try to forgive yourself for loving a person who could never become what you deserved. You have to find peace in understanding that the end is always a new beginning for you.

———————————————

Let us run away together. Let us run toward the love we've been afraid of, the type of romance that lives in dreams. The kind of love we've never known or seen.

Self-love is the way you hold yourself while weeping, mourning the death of a relationship that could never live up to what it means to be adequately loved by someone else.

———————————

Crying is a way for the soul to be set free from prison.

There are many paths to self-love. If one road doesn't work, you can always reroute, change direction.

You may be different after you get through this, but you will always be you, just a newer version and possibly stronger.

Just because you're durable doesn't mean you should stay with someone who wishes to break you down.

———————————————————

You have the right to change your mind, even when your heart is being stubborn. You can imagine leaving even when your legs refuse to move.

How long this will hurt is not your decision, but surviving is a choice.

She'd wander, but she was never lost. She just enjoyed the way it felt to feel freedom in the wind and the world at her back.

Reality is a prison for the dreamers.

———————

Often, there is nothing different about exes. They return pretending to be new, but they still taste like the past. They always feel like the thing you were eager to leave behind.

At the end, when this is over, I hope I'm the one who forgets, because there is nothing I'd like to remember.

You said that maybe one day we could try again, and a part of me got offended because it almost seemed as if you believed that my future would somehow be a loss without you, but here I am, in the future. And here I am thriving without you.

_____

It's just that sometimes people aren't cut out to fit the empty spaces in your life, and in the end, you realize that there is no forcing the wrong people into areas they're not suited to occupy.

How glad I am to know what it means to get hurt, stumble, and fall.
Only to pick myself up from the ground after it all.

You can be your sanctuary as soon as you realize that you are more than enough.

Someone will genuinely love you, and right now, that someone is you.

Move forward so that when they come back, you will no longer be where they left you.

If where you are is hurting you, find some other place to be.

Stop offering things to people who make you feel like it is never
enough.

He didn't leave you because you weren't enough. He left because you were more than he could ever deserve, and he was incapable of matching your devotion.

Some love is a manuscript that never deserved to be published.

One day you'll look behind you and see all the things you thought you'd never get over.

You thought life would end, and you believed that you could never move forward, but look how far you've come. Look how much further you are from the pain and how close you've come to the realization that there is more, something better out there for you.

_____

There are billions of hearts in the world, and yours is worth being found by someone worthy of you.

She lives as if the word "limitation" has no meaning. She makes the impossible seem like a joke. She is and will forever be more significant than anything placed in her way. She is you.

When it happens, when it's true. The love and understanding will come easy.

———————————————

The hailstorm in my heart has been transformative. Our inability to coexist has put me on a path that keeps me further away from you, and maybe there's salvation in this exile. Perhaps the only way to begin this love story is in the wake of our ending.

We'd trade in the lonely nights for restless conversation if the universe allowed it. We're only apart now because we're too stubborn to leave behind those who were never worthy of our emotions—tirelessly trying in search of a sign of life—holding on to the ghosts of empty promises—keeping one another waiting while we pretend to be happy with all the sorrow in our hearts.

————————————————

Sometimes you lose people so that something better can take their place.

You can get upset, but that doesn't mean you're an angry person. People will label you angry when you've adequately reacted to their improper treatment of you and your heart. They'll label you to silence you from responding in a way that they are not comfortable with, but I say fuck that. Be mad and feel whatever it is you need to feel because, to feel peace, you must make room for it and make room for peace by being honest about what they made you feel. Just don't stay in the space of anger; do not surrender your emotional power to a feeling that is only meant to remain temporary. You being upset is valid, but staying in that emotion is like standing proudly in quicksand.

It's awful; it hurts, but when your heart comes crashing down, you'll pick up the pieces, and you'll rebuild it to withstand better whatever heartache comes.

There is a solitude of strength that can only be discovered once you journey out alone, moving further away from all the people who doubt your magic. And though that path is a tough one, you will prove to be greater than any obstacle that sits in your way.

we began to wilt

like rose petals

being kissed

by winter's wind

isn't it time to go

daylight fades beside a full moon

draping us in darkness

hidden from one another

———————————

crying, shedding the hate

shedding the weight of sadness

removing sorrow, making room for peace

——————————————

the night can never stop the sun from shining

and the day can't stand in the way of the moon

chapter four
by Samantha King Holmes

I hope your love is intoxicating
Tangled in the sheets
That trust, compromise, and endurance
are stitched into the framework
A calm reassurance that
becomes your stronghold in life
A simple truth
That he saw you and understood that
You are good
You are enough
Deserving of a lifetime of love
that he is only beginning to show you

My hope is that you stop letting fear
control the narrative and give into the possibility

No one likes change
Growth takes sacrifice
This is just the uncomfortable part
Your bloom is going to be amazing

I hope you find the strength to remove
people from your life who don't give you
a chance to show there's more to you than
your low moments

I think we confuse forgiveness with continuing to allow someone toxic to be in our lives. Forgiving someone and deciding to no longer associate with that person is perfectly reasonable. The truth is some people just don't change. We hope they will, but that's not something that is in our control. Sometimes who someone is, even if we disagree with their behavior, needs to be accepted. We have to stop trying to make people out of whom we want them to be. This isn't limited to relationships; it's all interactions. Accepting someone doesn't mean you continue to allow them to be in your life. It's just looking at something from a realistic standpoint and making a conscious decision based on that. We have limits, and there is nothing wrong with setting firm boundaries. At some point, you realize you don't want to pretend like it's ok that someone treated you poorly. You don't have to.

There is a freedom that comes
from not seeking the validation of others
Now, all the important work starts

We don't focus enough on what truly brings us joy outside of the relationships we create. You should be able to feel happiness outside of them. I think we've become dependent on other people to provide that for us without even knowing what it looks like for ourselves. What is it that fills you up every day? Where is the fulfillment in your life? We spend so much time getting to know people. Make sure you're taking time to focus on yourself as well and what it is you truly want out of life.

I don't think we're always honest about what it is that we need. We sometimes hold on to people because we're looking for something more and decide to let them be in our company till we find it. We don't admit the things loneliness compels us to do. If we were forced to take a long, hard look at the many relationships we have in our lives, we would find that we don't really get much from them. I'm not into empty connections or holding on to anything that doesn't fill me up. Be wary of holding on for the sake of it.

I have made people my source of happiness
It's a shameful truth that I have only begun to admit
I've allowed others to fill me with joy
When they stopped, I simply moved on
to the next person who uplifted my spirits
I didn't once question why I was so distressed alone
I have treated people as if they were magic
trapped in my veins
making their way in and out of my heart
They were never the cure
Just beautiful distractions who prolonged the inevitable

Feeling betrayed by someone you once trusted is a hard thing to get past. You question how you couldn't see that they were capable of it or couldn't acknowledge that there were red flags that you chose to ignore because you liked being with them. It makes you take a step back and start asking if there were other things you didn't realize or whether someone else in your life would be capable of doing that. We tend to blame ourselves when someone does us wrong, despite their actions being their choice. It makes you not want to trust people moving forward. Give yourself a break. Don't shut yourself out from the world. The people who betrayed you already damaged your outlook; don't allow them the opportunity to stop you from being open to something beautiful making its way into your life.

I think you know what's going on
have a gut feeling
You won't say it out loud
won't question it
You know the moment you do
the truth will destroy this lie
you've been living
Don't wait too long to face it

It takes a lot to sit and process something that you'd rather not think about. I get that. The issue with that is not being able to take in the lesson life has now offered you and allowing yourself to fold into another situation just like it. We question how we're always the one giving and the people we choose to be around are just takers. Well, when was the first time that happened? When it happened a second time, did you do anything differently? I think it's hard for us to wrap our minds around why the same things keep happening without stopping and realizing that the common denominator in those situations is us. We're choosing these people; we're continuing to ignore certain behavior. I understand you don't like to think about the painful parts of your past and to sit in that discomfort, but you don't realize the pain you could be saving yourself from if you did.

You have to give yourself more credit than that. We put others so high on a pedestal that we don't recognize that they're the ones losing out on all that we have to offer. We act as if we're not the gift. Someone worth working to keep. The truth is what we're running from is bigger than them; they just happen to benefit from fear restricting us. Stop acting like you're beneath others, and don't let them feel like they have that over you. If it feels like you cherish someone more than they cherish you, ask yourself why you aren't looking for someone who gives you the same energy.

It seems worth it in the moment
Feeding the impulse
The way back down isn't so enticing
The next hour, next day, two weeks later
The guilt starts to creep in
The reality that the time, effort, compromise
all the trust that was built
wasn't worth the split-second choice
that it took to destroy it

It's hard to trust people. It gets even harder when someone you put your trust in takes advantage of it. After that, it seems like everyone is going to do the same thing, even when they aren't. Your guard goes up full throttle. Betrayal takes away more than just trust. It steals your peace of mind and ability to be vulnerable moving forward. So, before you think about making a selfish decision, consider the totality of the damage.

I'm not a hoarder of things but of people
So used to abandonment that
when someone good crosses my path
I let them pile up, even though
I'm sure my heart has no more space

Her love for him was formidable
embedded into her being
She rooted him deep down into her core
She felt whole
Over time, their love faltered
She knew she had to carve
a piece of herself out
in order to be free of him
For him to be free of her

That's what it feels like, every time
For all that people give
It's the pieces they take with them
that we are left without
that don't ever seem to get replenished

I feel like such a fraud
I tell you to be strong
while most days
I feel like I'm one push away
from crumbling
I've been holding my breath
waiting for the impact
Please excuse my silence
It is hard enough trying to hold it together
without having to also carry your pain

The things that we claim break us actually build our character. None of us like going through those experiences, but we gain so much knowledge from them. All those stories, bruised feelings, sleepless nights shape who we are. I may not like what I've been through, but I like who I am and who I'm becoming. That, to me, is worth sharing without shame.

It is better to be an active participant in your healing process rather than hope that one day things will just magically be different. I've found that letting go and moving forward are difficult concepts for people. You linger on thoughts of "what if" and keep yourself in this state of mind in which any movement forward seems impossible. The reason things didn't work and the flaws that you know are there are completely disregarded. Take hold of your self-worth and your future. I'm not going to tell you that everything is going to be ok tomorrow. It may not feel that way. I will tell you that it is a process, but it's better to be on that journey than remaining stagnant. Life has too much to offer you to waste it in a space in which you aren't growing.

We like what's familiar. We cling to it, as the mere thought of change is scary. We hold on to all the routine moments that bring us temporary joy: date nights, texts in the morning, the sweet moments that get captured. We live in these and try to disregard the larger pockets of time when we aren't actually happy. Once we walk away, we know that our time will now be filled with a large void and relentless obsession over how things went so wrong. It's a shame that it hasn't been figured out yet, that moving on doesn't have to be this agonizing process. Yes, when you care for someone and are with them for a long time, it hurts when it ends. The hardest part is being able to show yourself that you can live without them. The thing is you can, though. You already have, and moving forward, you will.

I knew I shouldn't have stayed
I just couldn't find it in me to leave
So, I went out and sought pleasure
It wasn't worth my integrity

Not everyone you meet, date, or get into a relationship with is going to be "the one." That's also a lot of pressure to put on a relationship early on. I think we give too much too soon a lot of the time. We don't give people the chance to show us they can be trusted or are worth doting on. We just tell ourselves how the relationship could be, and despite the flags that come, we push through because we have already created the fantasy of the "perfect relationship." There is no such thing. Healthy relationships take work, compromise, good communication, and the ability to grow with a person. We get so caught up in the time we invested that we hold on even when we're not happy. I get that there's this whole notion of not letting go because you don't want the next person to benefit from all the turmoil you were put through. Though, the truth is that if someone is treating you poorly, that is your reality. You can't try to create one with a different outcome.

Is there no solace for the meek and wounded?
I've given myself without restriction to others
Honest in my intention
Only to be left deprived of love and betrayed
Is that not enough of a penance?
I also must be plagued by the
false dreams they painted for me
Am I not allowed a moment of reprieve?
I didn't know I could miss the comfort of silence
I'd give anything to simply be still
immersed in nothing more than
the comfort of my chair
and the weight of my body within it

He makes me feel like I'm not good enough
No matter how many times
or the different ways I tell him so
he still does it
It's my fault for allowing him
to have an input in my self-esteem

I've been searching for in others
what I can't find in myself
Give me your confidence, your bravery
your sweet love and devotion
I've made man my religion
No wonder I'm coming up empty
Spiraling from time spent being led
by those who are just as lost as I am

I don't know how to get back to myself
So, I'm reaching out for you to save me
I know it won't work
You can't mend the broken pieces
Your touch doesn't reach that deep
Your love has been a slow drip
trying to fill a bottomless hole
I just want to stay in bed
I guess that means it's catching up
A hand touch away from consuming me
In endless days of being buried in my covers
longingly looking for a way out

No matter how good you are
The bad decisions you've made
tend to find you
It's humbling
It's life's way of lending an opportunity
to not seek vengeance
but to reconcile with the pain you caused
hopefully to never do it again

Lessons, so many lessons. It's interesting how easy it is to detach from something that was once thought of as too hard to move forward from. I mean relentlessly obsessing over, days locked away doing nothing. Now it is nothing more than a moment in time that can be recalled, relayed, and learned from. Funny how life works. The things we think are going to destroy us teach us about ourselves and others. I can go back and remember how it felt during that time. I can pen it out, but there is no need for me to look back and dwell on it. Just take it for what it was and let that be.

You know when you get to that point when you don't want to talk about the situation anymore. Your friends are tired of hearing about it. You're in a space where you feel like you have no one to talk to, and you're wondering how you even got there. You don't have to be there. Don't put being with someone over your peace of mind.

Some people impact our lives so deeply it feels like we've known them the whole time. As if they are extensions of ourselves. I've had to learn that the good that someone can bring out in you doesn't just disappear because they are no longer in your life. Some people make us brave, believe in ourselves, and see all the beauty that we couldn't see in ourselves before. Someone no longer being a part of your life in no way diminishes the impact. People have their purpose and season within our lives. Allow what they brought out in you to be the gift it is.

chapter five
by r.h. Sin

I know you've been thinking that you're on your own, alone in a valley of sadness, tirelessly running from everything you wish you could forget. I know you believe that you may not have been worthy of the things you've wanted, and now you're out here attempting to find meaning within the heartache you've struggled with. I won't lie to you: the road will be long, it'll be rough, and there will come a time when you'll struggle to see what's in front of you. But I promise you this: if you keep going, if you continue to put distance between yourself and all the people who hurt you, you'll find that when the rain stops, you'll have pushed yourself to be closer to everything you truly deserve.

———————————————

It's okay to hit "unfollow" on the people you know in real life.

———————————

It is only when you distance yourself from certain people that you know when to stay and when to leave.

Take care of all the things you want to last, and walk away from anyone who doesn't care for you.

His mixed signals are screaming "no." Please stay away from men who are confused about what they feel for you.

Good moments can exist in the darkest of days.

At some point, you realize that people decide to do certain things even when they know they'll break your heart if and when you find out. Mistakes shouldn't be repeated, and what is done by them to you is simply because they don't give a fuck.

———————————

Relationships aren't always easy, but no relationship worth staying in feels like hell.

When you begin to wonder if you should stay, this is when you
know you should go.

———————————

Forgive her, the younger version of you.

You are a bouquet of roses; give them to yourself.

You've been watering dead plants for far too long, and it's time that you turn your devotion inward.

You've felt too much and too often for the wrong people, and so it's okay to feel nothing for no one.

You will never find love by going back to an ex who left you to fuck someone else.

Some lose themselves; others change. And maybe a different you will emerge from these flames, stronger than before.

You didn't want closure. I believe you just wanted to see him. You were hoping to get a glimpse of him, the idea that maybe you missed a reason to stay. You were hoping that perhaps he'd take this last chance at seeing you and say something that'll make you regret leaving, but it's the same old story. No matter how hard you try to rewrite it, things come out the same. You were always deserving of more, and he will never be the person to give it to you.

Holding on to the hand of someone who makes you feel like you're unworthy is prolonged suffering. Inside you lives the power of choice, the decision to say no to everyone who doesn't deserve a yes.

I think I was afraid of being alone, but in that fear, I didn't realize that giving my time to the wrong person was the actual recipe for loneliness. I kept looking for pieces of good amid the rubble of chaos and confusion. Telling myself that if I stayed a bit longer, things would somehow transform from a disaster's disfigurement that the relationship had become. You tell yourself whatever you can; you make excuses daily to keep yourself stuck on a roller coaster that is filled with more downs than ups and that will eventually lead to nowhere. This is what we've all been guilty of doing, filling our heads and hearts with stories that are ultimately the ones we want to read but ignoring the fact that everything we've written about the person we're with is a complete work of fiction and the ending will always hurt no matter the realization. I reached the conclusion of leaving because staying would have eventually kept me distracted from not only finding love but also loving myself. I hope you get there. I hope these words serve as a reminder of not only what you've been through but where you can go after.

You speak love into your life as soon as you voice the words "I'm choosing myself."

To fall in love with someone obsessed with acts that will make your heart smile. That is a love you've hoped for.

You were living for yourself before he ever had a chance to waste a moment of your time, and when this is finally over, you'll do what you were doing before you met him. You will live and love yourself.

It's not love if you relate to the painful words in this book. It's not love if it hurts this bad.

I thought about you the other day and the way you sway back and forth within the storm's eye, refusing to break. You may bend to the wind, gracefully bowing to the pressure, but you refuse to come undone by this chaos in motion. There are moments when onlookers sit to witness what they believe will be your end, but you find new ways to put yourself back together again as soon as the storm passes. You grow through every season, you survive every storm, which is why I believe in you.

Letting go is a skill set acquired by the heart of a person who no longer wishes to love people and things that no longer serve them peace.

The reward of seeing beyond your current heartache and the people who hurt you is that there is something beautiful awaiting you whenever you're ready to move forward. It's so easy to get stuck in spaces because of the time spent. It's easy to become numb to the negativity when you're used to it, but deep down, you know that something better is calling out. And if you look hard enough, if you look further into the distance, you'll see that a better you, a much stronger you, is reaching out in your direction. Let go of what's keeping you in a pit of sadness, and reach toward yourself and the love you've always been capable of providing.

When the beauty of all things vanishes, look into a mirror to re-create it.

I could always see myself falling in love with the heart of a woman whose eyes seem so weary from losing sleep over lovers who could never love her.

The truth is your decision to leave is just your way of being honest with yourself.

You will break several times on your way to self-love and the romance that can only be had in a relationship worthy of everything you went through to get there.

I wanted the type of love that felt like escaping the city for the lakes and mountains of nature.

This will pass. The pain you feel right now is only temporary, and, sooner or later, you'll find your way out.

How long before the fire burns in your favor? There will come a day where you won't be bothered by the smoke, and you'll see the flames as a triumph. For you will have learned to set fire to those things that used to hurt you.

There's a type of beauty in solitude, but you have to be okay with being alone to witness it.

———————

The rain starts, and it reminds you that it's okay to cry. It's okay to let it go, and it's okay to let it fall.

The scars of a survivor are art etched in the skin: a warrior's tattoo, a triumph.

I know you're hurting. I wish there were something I could say to you to chase the pain away. This is not the first time you've felt like this, and it won't be the last. You have always found ways to survive; there's an art to the way you fight. The way you overcome the heartache is a poem within itself, and I hope you find a way to get through this.

You know what you deserve; you know what you've been fighting for, and I know it's been a long journey, but please, keep going. I believe in you. Believe in yourself, even on your worst days.

She was always running from the truth, lying to herself while standing beneath storm clouds. She was forcing her lips to smile even when there were tears in her eyes. I think she's known all along that sadness had known her name and where to find her, but a part of her believed that if she pretended to be okay long enough, everything would change, but it didn't.

I wonder what the days of tomorrow will gift you for surviving. Sometimes I wonder what you'll be rewarded for choosing to continue to fight for all that you deserve. May the rain be a little lighter and the sun gentle on your skin. May your nights be a bit easier and the moon a bit brighter as you navigate the darkness.

It took me years to understand the real value of letting go. It took me years to realize that sometimes absence can be a gift, and the more I walked away from certain people, the closer I was to peace and happiness. You see, some people bring with them a storm, and the sun is only visible whenever they leave and or whenever you leave them behind. I know letting go is something you've struggled with, but I think it's vital to see the reward. Look at it like this: everything you could ever want is hidden behind the people who hurt you, even those who claim to love but often leave you in tears. There is a paradise to be found by those who detach from the people who hurt them. And it's time to choose yourself.

Do not waste your moon's light on those who would rather see you struggle in the dark. Do not waste the warmth of your flames on those who would rather see you run cold. Do not waste your love on people who act as if they hate you.

Look at where you've come from; you've traveled so damn far, and you only ever look back for clarity. Everything that was left behind is a testament to your dedication to looking forward to more. Be proud of yourself and your ability to survive. Be proud of the fact that somehow you rediscovered the light that lives within you and that same light will lead you to everything you deserve.

You ran out of daylight, and so you burned bridges to see; you burned bridges to find a better path to take.

I know you're afraid of being alone, but doesn't loneliness plague your heart whenever it is given to certain people? If a room is filled with the wrong people, you are likely to feel empty. And this is where you are, struggling with letting go of all the people who were never worthy of being kept. The freedom you seek can only be achieved after you've moved on. The peace you've always wanted can only take shape in the absence of those who stir up a kind of chaos in your soul. And you will never dream of heaven the way you wish, lying beside the devil.

Awaken from your dreams by a nightmare reality. You are your happiest when you drift into a delightful abyss. You do not know the face of joy until you've closed your eyes, and everything you've always wanted lives in a dreamscape.

I wonder if our shadows feel our pain, or do they only witness our shattered dreams, always following close behind us even when we're headed for hell and heartbreak.

I'm speaking to you over the noise, hoping my words bypass the lies that you've been told. You join me here whenever your heart begins to break; you consume each word because you're tired of the emptiness you feel inside. You're hungry for more, and that is the first step to letting go. The realization that there is something greater awaiting you when you exit out of the door and go down the path of peace. A road that leads you further from the person you wish could love you. It won't be easy; it never is, and it was never meant to be, but to rediscover the heaven that lives within, you have to decide that you don't deserve the hell they've put you through.

Dear stranger, I know you. I resonate with what you're feeling right now as you read this. I have spent the better part of my life wishing to be seen and heard. My voice is not loud enough to match or overshadow my heart's sounds as it breaks into a million pieces. I was led astray and often led to hell, as the person I could have done everything for did everything in their power to break me.

There's been something I've been meaning to tell you, and I've waited for the perfect time. In this moment, you've nearly reached the end of your rope, and what you may not have known is that somewhere inside your bones lives the energy to create an extension that will buy you more time as you restart the journey of carrying yourself further away from the traumas of sharing your divine energy with those who will never appreciate it for what it is. You've spent so much time in the deep end that you have forgotten to reach for your hand. You've been looking for a sign outside of yourself when, all this time, the answers have always lived within you. It's time to redirect the energy you've used to hold on and give it to the healing process. Anything that does not serve your ideas of being happy should be left behind.

Let the tears flow, and empty yourself of everything that's been breaking you down. You'll find rest in the mourning of everything you thought you needed. Cry and empty yourself so that all that is left is you, because all that you need is you.

You've spent so many years looking for someone to share your melody with that you've forgotten the importance of singing for yourself.

Maybe the heartbreak is just a chaotic transformation into strength and the courage to continue toward the most beautiful relationship you could ever have.

———————————

Heartbreak happens, but it leaves you open for something better. They go, but that sets you free. You may not have seen it this way, and I know it doesn't feel like it, but their absence means more freedom to choose yourself.

Midnights are tailored for the wandering soul in search of peace. Tonight, you and I hold hands as we venture out into the darkness with only the moon's light to lead us.

————————————————

Let's be sad tonight. The sorrow is a stepping-stone to joy, so let's continue to climb.

I was cheated on by someone I did everything for, and maybe this is why I'm speaking to you. I know what it feels like to have a home filled with memories and hope, burned down by betrayal and selfishness. I know that lost feeling that occurs when you reach the end and are clueless about where you'll go to next or how you'll even get to where you wish to be. I know your pain; I know your disappointment. I think we've always related to a level of sadness, which brings us closer even as strangers. I'm writing to you because I know you by way of being broken.

———————————————

It would seem as if you're always waiting for the right time to pack up your things and vacate the space that is no longer deserving of your essence. You've considered leaving before, but there's something about this time that feels so different. You've been listening to your heart song lately, and you hear the sadness in the melodies; you hear the sorrow that seeps from the cracks in your heart. And I think you're fed up with the same old stories of how badly it hurts to love a person who appears to be incapable of reciprocating everything you've given unto them. You're approaching that point of breaking, that point of no return, and you finally understand that letting go is the first step to pointing yourself in the right direction. There's no longer a willingness to fracture your life with the weight of their mistreatment. No longer a need to extinguish your fire that had burned brighter before they entered your life.

No one tells the moon where to sit at midnight, and no one controls the sun's choice to shine its light. Be the moon during the night and the sun when it's morning. Do not allow anyone the power to dictate your want to rise; do not allow anyone the choice of deciding how you exist in this world.

She wrote it down in journals because she had no one to talk to, and so those pages became ears, listening without judgment. She wrote it down, all the things she wanted to scream, each word yelling out from the book's pages that most people didn't deserve to read. I'm in awe as she sat with sorrow, expressing her heavy truths on brittle lines, composing her story without limitations. She found a place where she could be honest about her soul's sadness, and I think that's brave. The courage to get it out, the strength to find a way to survive.

There's this battle going on within yourself. You are literally at war with the person looking back at you in the mirror. On the one hand, you're in love, and on the other, you hate the fact that you feel deeply for someone so shallow. You get to this place by believing the words of a liar. Someone wearing a mask, someone pretending to be the person you've always dreamed of. And for some time, that person was capable of living up to your initial expectations of what love could be. Here you are, trying to process your feelings of love and betrayal all at once, confused at what you should do. Searching for excuses to stay when leaving would be the best choice. What's fucked up about all of this is your struggle to see a future without this one person, who will destroy your life if you're unwilling to let go. You keep telling yourself that things will change; you search for the good times amid the rubble. You try to stand firm upon all the good memories, but even those moments aren't strong enough to support you. Each day harder than the last as you continue to run from your emotional truths, but the tears keep flowing and your heart continues to drown. There's no boat strong enough to resist sinking while drifting through waters of emotional uncertainty. But you keep trying, and you'll try some more. Yes, you'll try until you figure out a way to redirect your energy. You'll continue to fight for that person until you realize that there is nothing to gain by going into battle with someone who isn't concerned with being your ally. You'll keep trying until you know that your love story cannot truly begin to be written until you move forward without the person you thought would love you.

You must have forgotten about the way the sun rises just so that it could be in a position to witness your arrival as you awaken from your dreams. Jealous of the moon and the stars that get to stand outside your window, on guard as you sleep.

Some days are more challenging than most; some nights are darker than ever, but you find new ways to discover the path closest to survival. Another day, another moment to walk with the sun. Another night, a new opportunity to find your strength amid the darkness.

It takes time. You're learning how to heal your wounds. You're learning how to stand even when the foundation beneath your feet begins to break, trying to survive everything bound to perish. Take your time to find balance as you search for more reasons to move on with your life. Take your time to recover from the damnation of loving the wrong person.

The pain is just a moment before the joy. It is easier to see the rainbow after the storm ends. So wait; be patient.

To remain in the arms of a liar, you have to tell more lies than the person lying to you whenever you speak to yourself. Forcing your mind's sight beyond the truth and choosing to focus on the moments that make you want to stay.

When the day is without light and the clouds begin to cry and every moment of your existence is filled with a melancholy hue, do not forget to love yourself. Do not forget that even when alone, you are your best company. You are more than enough.

It was morning, and the moon stuck around a little longer, with hopes of catching the sun rise. That's love, defying all logic and reason just to witness someone ascend. Take a lover who will do anything to see you shine.

I think it's beautifully tragic how the stars find a way to shine even in death, keeping the night sky lit and complementing the moon. Helping the lost find their way through the darkness.

I believe in you. You have been here before, and you always find your way out. And it would be best if you were given all the credit for saving yourself, and I am just a mirror helping you reflect. Day to day, night after night, you struggle to survive, but you do it, and I just wanted to take this time to acknowledge you and your efforts. Thank you for always being brave enough to be honest with what you feel. It is your desire and search for more that have inspired what you're reading right now. As I've said before, I only wish to help somehow, and maybe these words will somehow help you rediscover everything you may have thought you lost. There's a woman reading this right now searching for a sign. I say to you, do not be afraid of the loneliness that may come when you detach from the things and people that hurt you. Do not be scared to start over alone and or with someone else. Before you choose to be with someone else, make sure you spend some time with yourself, some much-needed time to reflect on your life and what has happened and what you'll be looking for going forward. Knowing what you deserve and knowing what you should avoid will go hand in hand as you go off on a self-love journey. You can't force a man to feel a love that he is not strong enough to express. You can't force a man to be the type of man who deserves to be loved by you. You can't force a relationship to work when it was built on broken promises and betrayal. You can't waste your time on a relationship that keeps you distracted from finding the right person. It would be best if you weren't fighting for someone who uses their energy to fight you. You can't continue to try for someone who rarely makes an effort. You will never find peace in a relationship with someone comfortable with chaos. You dream of real love, but you're with the very person representing a nightmare, a cold, dark vision of everything you should avoid. Please consider this. The longer you stay with the wrong person, the further you are from knowing what it means to be loved romantically by someone outside of yourself. Self-love first, heal, figure out what you need and deserve by remembering how it felt to be with the wrong person. I'm just hoping these words will reach the one who needs it the most.

Dear Reader,

My mind ran off on you the other day, you, the stranger reading these words. I speak to you with familiarity, like we're close friends, because in a way we are. We are connected by heartache, forged together by the heartbreak. I don't know why I even bother at times, afraid that you'll overlook this note altogether, or maybe we're here together, this moment resonating with the both of us. I don't know why the midnight moon chose us to be restless under a weary sky, and I don't get how the both of us could be so kind to people who would only end up hurting our hearts. I was much younger when it began, but it got old fast. I continued fighting for something that they were unwilling to give, but I gave in hopes of changing their minds, and maybe we're just alike because of that one thing. The way we are eager to provide despite the other person's inability to reciprocate. Perhaps you're there now; maybe you're experiencing a breaking in your heart, but something in me knows that you will overcome it. I mastered seas of struggle and pain, swimming to a shore made of myself, and that's how you'll get through. You'll read these words, and you'll know that I was talking to you, and then you'll do what needs to be done; you will find a way back to yourself. Say this to yourself out loud . . . "I can, and I will make it over this mountain of hurt." Thank you for fucking with my words and allowing me space and time to express this to you. These words are my only way of communicating with you whenever I feel that it's time to connect. Now, go, be great. Be everything you know yourself to be. It's time to move forward. It's time to heal. It's time to be loved the way you deserve to be loved.

Sincerely, r.h. Sin

index
by r.h. Sin

I keep thinking about how people hold on to their phones as if they are genuinely a part of their being; in fact, I believe that this device has become more important than the people it promised to help us all stay in contact with.   60

I know they describe love as a spark or fireworks, but to be honest, I felt a bomb of emotion going off in my heart and throughout my bones when you touched me.   48

I know you're afraid of being alone, but doesn't loneliness plague your heart whenever it is given to certain people?   287

I know you're hurting.   279

I know you've been thinking that you're on your own, alone in a valley of sadness, tirelessly running from everything you wish you could forget.   244

I like to think of you when my skies are gray; there's just something about envisioning your face that makes this shit feel okay.   70

I'm confident that there is beauty behind that mask that hides your scars.   14

I'm not telling you to stop singing, I'm just trying to let you know that not everyone deserves your song.   10

I'm sorry, but I wish to interrupt you from that sadness you've been feeling.   156

I'm speaking to you over the noise, hoping my words bypass the lies that you've been told.   290

In all my years of living, I've reached the understanding that anger moves the body backward; it keeps the heart stuck and makes the soul restless.   120

In a way, you're a flower because of the simple fact that most people will never truly comprehend and or understand the value of your presence until the feelings you felt for them fade.   133

isn't it time to go   208

I think I fell in love with her soul first and the well-being of her heart.   51

I think it's beautifully tragic how the stars find a way to shine even in death, keeping the night sky lit and complementing the moon.   310

I think I was afraid of being alone, but in that fear, I didn't realize that giving my time to the wrong person was the actual recipe for loneliness.   261

I think nightclubs are just shelters for the lonely.   171

I thought about you the other day and the way you sway back and forth within the storm's eye, refusing to break.   266

It is only when you distance yourself from certain people that you know when to stay and when to leave.   246

It made ruins of my heart, loving you.   78

It never needed to be perfect, and I just wanted to feel like I mattered as much as you did to me.   144

It rained, and she wasn't looking for an umbrella.   26

It's awful; it hurts, but when your heart comes crashing down, you'll pick up the pieces, and you'll rebuild it to withstand better whatever heartache comes.   205

It's hard to move on when you're stuck with the idea of what you're leaving behind.   135

index
by R.M. Drake

index
by Samantha King-Holmes

Andrews McMeel Publishing
a division of Andrews McMeel Universal
1130 Walnut Street, Kansas City, Missouri 64106

www.andrewsmcmeel.com

21 22 23 24 25 RR2 10 9 8 7 6 5 4 3 2 1

ISBN: 978-1-5248-6538-2

Library of Congress Control Number: 2021930963

Editor: Patty Rice
Art Director/Designer: Diane Marsh
Production Editor: Elizabeth A. Garcia
Production Manager: Cliff Koehler

ATTENTION: SCHOOLS AND BUSINESSES
Andrews McMeel books are available at quantity discounts
with bulk purchase for educational, business, or sales
promotional use. For information, please e-mail the Andrews
McMeel Publishing Special Sales Department: specialsales@
amuniversal.com.